TO:

FROM:

theCouponCollection

SOURCEBOOKS, INC.
NAPERVILLE, ILLINOIS

The Perfect GEMINI Coupons

A coupon gift to inspire the best in you

 SOURCEBOOKS, INC.
NAPERVILLE, ILLINOIS

Copyright © 2004 by Sourcebooks, Inc.
Cover and internal design © 2004 by Sourcebooks, Inc.
Cover and internal illustration © 2004 Anne Crosse
Sourcebooks and the colophon are registered trademarks of Sourcebooks, Inc.

All rights reserved. No part of this book may be reproduced in any form or by any electronic or mechanical means including information storage and retrieval systems—except in the case of brief quotations embodied in critical articles or reviews—without permission in writing from its publisher, Sourcebooks, Inc.

Published by Sourcebooks, Inc.
P.O. Box 4410, Naperville, Illinois 60567-4410
(630) 961-3900
FAX: (630) 961-2168
www.sourcebooks.com

ISBN 1-4022-0184-2

Printed and bound in the United States of America

AP 10 9 8 7 6 5 4 3 2 1

THE PERFECT GEMINI
Born May 21 – June 21

Welcome to the world of the perfect Gemini. Astrology is a powerful symbolic language for describing and interpreting human life and events on the Earth. This coupon book is a fun way to dip into that ancient pool of knowledge and make the most of the potential that lies in your nature.

WHY ASTROLOGY?

Astrologers believe that the makeup, configuration, and movement of the planets and stars correspond with events anywhere in the universe, including human lives, and that studying these cycles can help people understand the past and present, and even predict the future. By mapping the position of the other planets in our galaxy, the moon, and the sun in the heavens when you were born, astrology finds indications of the circumstances you may encounter, as well as clues to your basic personality traits and how you relate to others.

THE TWELVE HOUSES

Imagine a wheel in space that circles the Earth like a cigar band. This band is divided into twelve sections, or houses, because the sun spends approximately one month in each area in relationship to the Earth, as our planet makes its yearly journey around the sun. (In ancient times, of course, it was believed that the sun was, in fact, circling the Earth.) The wheel of the Zodiac divides the heavens into the twelve traditional astrological groupings, each of which is assigned certain polarities, qualities, and elements. The Zodiac wheel also makes clear the relationships among the signs. For instance, Gemini is located on the wheel directly opposite the sign of Sagittarius, and is in many ways the Archer's opposite in values and interests.

Although the location of the sun at the time of your birth—your sun sign—provides the basic key to your personality, in astrology, *each* of the planets in our galaxy, as well as the moon, has influences which are expressed in your life.

THE TWO POLARITIES

All the signs are divided into two polarities, either masculine or feminine types. The male signs are more active and extroverted, as in the Chinese philosophical term yang, which refers to the positive, bright, and masculine. The female signs are considered more sensitive, meditative, and inward looking, as in the Chinese yin, which is the negative, dark, and feminine. Of course, astrology has always acknowledged that everyone embodies both female and male energies in their nature.

As a Gemini, your essence is masculine. You have strong male traits in your essential nature, which will interact with all the cultural and societal influences you encounter, as well as the other influences in your astrological chart (for instance, the location of the moon at your birth).

THE THREE QUALITIES

A lesser known aspect of astrology divides the signs into three types of qualities—cardinal, fixed, or mutable—which have to do with how you relate to the world. The four cardinal signs (Aries, Cancer, Libra, and Capricorn) are the most assertive, the most interested in making changes, leading, and being in control. The four fixed signs (Taurus, Leo, Scorpio, and Aquarius) tend to resist outside influences, and are strong and stable at best, or stubborn and perverse at worst.

As a Gemini, you are one of the four mutable signs, along with Virgo, Sagittarius, and Pisces. You are the most changeable and open to outside influences. The good news is, you can be adaptable and versatile. The bad news is, you may tend toward instability, or over-compensate by being overly concerned with finding security.

THE FOUR ELEMENTS

Each sign of the Zodiac is also associated with one of the four elements: fire, earth, air, or water, which lend certain characteristics to those signs. The three fire signs are Aries, Leo, and Sagittarius—they tend to be energetic, impatient, explosive, and…well, fiery.

The three earth signs are Taurus, Virgo, and Capricorn. These earthy types are—you guessed it—down to earth. They tend to be practical, reliable, and cautious.

The emotional water signs are Cancer, Scorpio, and Pisces. These are the sensitive ones, the dreamers, the spiritualists. They are capable of great depths of emotion and compassion.

You, Gemini, are one of the air signs of the Zodiac, along with Libra and Aquarius. The air signs are the thinkers, the intellectuals, and the planners. Geminis, in particular, are known as the great communicators of the Zodiac. You are youthful and full of fresh ideas. You have no difficulty expressing your ideas—or influencing other people's.

YOUR RULING PLANETS

According to ancient astrology, the sun and moon ruled one house each, and the five other known planets (Mercury, Venus, Mars, Jupiter, and Saturn) ruled two houses each. As they were discovered, the farther distant planets of Uranus, Neptune, and

Pluto were added to the ancient system, resulting in some houses having a "secondary" ruler.

You, Gemini, are clearly ruled by the planet Mercury—the messenger god. As Mercury is associated with travel and communication, you tend to be exceptionally active, volatile, energetic, and motivated. Whatever your destination, you always want to get there quickly.

As an intellectual air sign, it is a Gemini's nature to be concerned with rational, logical thought and the gathering of information. The influence of Mercury stimulates the mind and allows you great cunning and achievement. However, you are easily bored and may be quite incapable of sticking to one thing at a time—Gemini is symbolized by the Heavenly Twins, representing the duality of your nature. You excel in careers where communication is key, such as writing, law, journalism, teaching, or computer programming.

Gemini is a masculine—positive, bright, outgoing—sign, and is very difficult to pin down. Remember, too, that Gemini is a mutable sign, which heightens the properties of Mercury and may lead you to be fickle and dissatisfied.

MIXING WITH THE OTHER ELEMENTS

With your quicksilver nature, you can use the support of the Earth signs (Taurus, Virgo, and Capricorn) for stability. You share particular empathy with Virgo, which is also ruled by Mercury. These friends, while they may seem a bit stodgy to you, will keep you grounded. They can help you gather your scattered and abundant ideas and see them through to completion.

Be careful around your Fire sign friends (Aries, Leo, and Sagittarius)—all your combined energy could be explosive. There's no lack of power, ambition, or enthusiasm here; if you can stay on track and keep from burning out, together you will change the world.

The combination of Air and Water creates some wild possibilities. Around the quiet, introspective Water signs (Cancer, Scorpio, and Pisces), Geminis may find themselves frustrated and at odds. However, if you can summon some patience, and allow yourself to be calmed and comforted, these elements balance each other nicely.

WHAT'S YOUR MOON?

The position of the moon at your birth exerts a strong influence on the basic elements of your Gemini personality. The house occupied by the Moon channels the expression of your personality in such areas as maternal qualities, domestic interests, and emotional needs.

For example, a moon in Scorpio brings a powerful emotional force to your sprightly Gemini nature: as a parent, your Gemini youthfulness will balance the Scorpio intensity, making you an enthusiastic and successful parent who loves to have fun with the family. In romance, a moon in Scorpio brings a great deal of passion to the intellectual rapport and taste for variety you exhibit as a Gemini, making you capable of a very fulfilling relationship. You may want to investigate how your sun sign is tempered by the other influences in your astrological chart—it's both entertaining and a rich source of imagery and meaning.

GEMINI IN LOVE

In general, Geminis tend to be versatile and lively, which can be wonderful in their personal relationships—as long as they don't become bored. Your wit and youthful energy make you a rewarding companion, although your restlessness can drive your partner crazy. At your best, you are eloquent, communicative, intelligent, and inventive. You might want to avoid people who bring out your possible tendencies to be nervous, inconsistent, and shallow. You are probably happiest with a partner who can keep up with your many, varied, and constantly changing interests, or at least tolerate them and enjoy the whirl!

Take a look at the coupons in this book; they are designed to help you explore your compatibility with other signs, bring out your best traits, and help you with your worst. Have a great time exploring the wisdom of the stars!

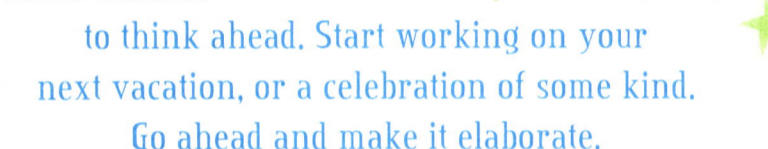

Since Geminis **LOVE TO PLAN,** now's the time to think ahead. Start working on your next vacation, or a celebration of some kind. Go ahead and make it elaborate.

Gemini and Aquarius make a great combination: Gemini loves variety, and Aquarius is just the one to supply it!

theCouponCollection

To help your Gemini airiness
GET A LITTLE GROUNDED,
try making something out of clay
or go and paint pottery.
You'll probably find this very soothing.

An earthy Virgo, who likes order, can provide the perfect balance for an airy Gemini, who loves movement, as long as they are tolerant of their differences.

theCouponCollection
SOURCEBOOKS, INC.
NAPERVILLE, ILLINOIS

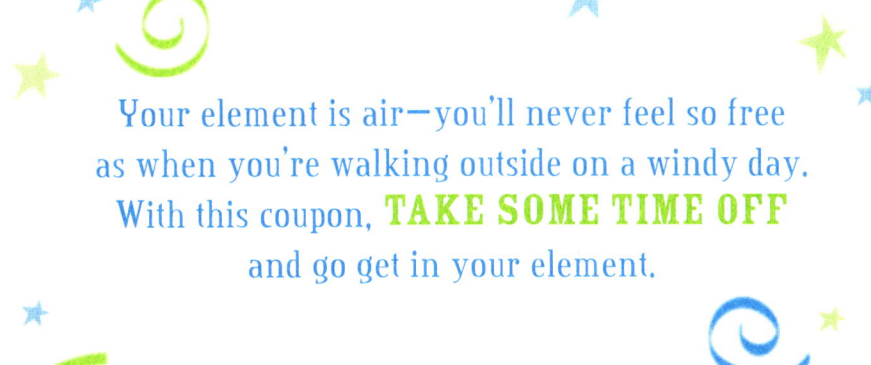

Your element is air—you'll never feel so free as when you're walking outside on a windy day. With this coupon, **TAKE SOME TIME OFF** and go get in your element.

A Gemini who hooks up with a Libra, another air sign, will find a companion who shares their love of freedom.

theCouponCollection

SOURCEBOOKS, INC.

While Gemini can be explosive when
coming into contact with a fire sign,
try bringing some of the warmth of the sun in,
without the volatility. On the next warm day,
lie down in the sun and
SOAK UP A FEW RAYS.

A fiery, energetic Aries and a spontaneous Gemini together make for a red-hot romance.

theCouponCollection
SOURCEBOOKS, INC.
NAPERVILLE, ILLINOIS

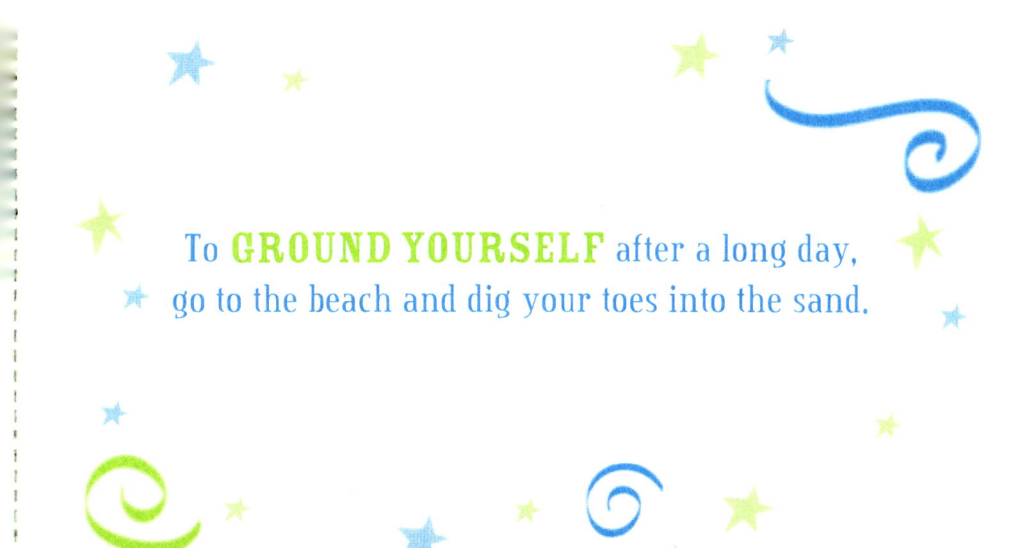

To **GROUND YOURSELF** after a long day, go to the beach and dig your toes into the sand.

The natural common sense and down-to-earth quality of a Virgo may be just right for balancing a restless Gemini.

theCouponCollection
SOURCEBOOKS, INC.
NAPERVILLE, ILLINOIS

You're **EXPRESSIVE** and **COMMUNICATIVE**—
why not express yourself by singing
at the top of your lungs?
This coupon entitles you to belt out one song
of your choice—either with the radio,
alone in the shower, or in front of friends!

When a happy-go-lucky Sagittarius teams up with a quicksilver Gemini, the results can be astonishing—just don't get arrested!

theCouponCollection

SOURCEBOOKS, INC.
NAPERVILLE, ILLINOIS

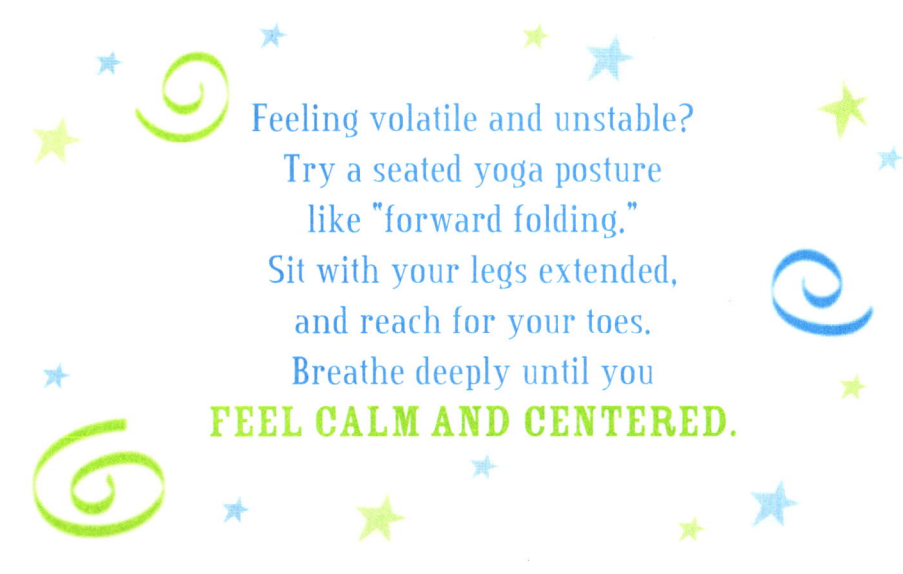

A sensitive, compassionate Cancer can provide the roving Gemini with a loving place to come home to.

theCouponCollection
SOURCEBOOKS, INC.
NAPERVILLE, ILLINOIS

EXPRESS your Gemini spirit—wear a diaphanous scarf or shawl.

The esoteric, dreamy Pisces paired with the daring Gemini will find no end of imaginative, creative fun.

theCouponCollection

SOURCEBOOKS, INC.
NAPERVILLE, ILLINOIS

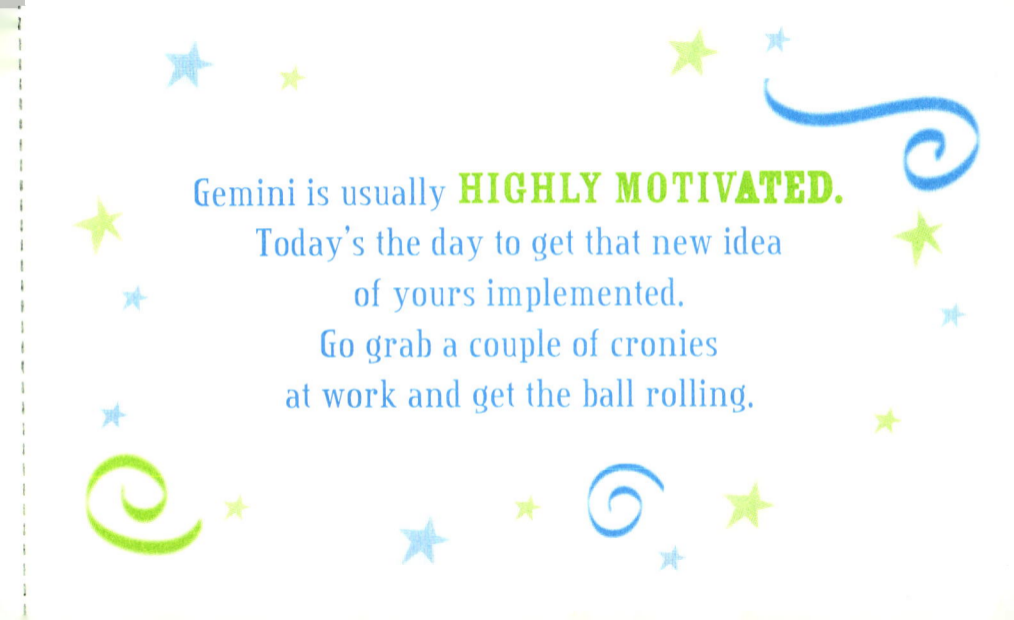

Gemini is usually **HIGHLY MOTIVATED.**
Today's the day to get that new idea
of yours implemented.
Go grab a couple of cronies
at work and get the ball rolling.

Hard-working, meticulous Virgo is the one that Gemini needs to help give those brilliant dreams some solid reality.

theCouponCollection

SOURCEBOOKS, INC.
NAPERVILLE, ILLINOIS

For a few minutes of Gemini peace,
lie on the ground and
GAZE UP AT THE CLOUDS.

When a high-flying Gemini and a knowledgeable Aquarius get together, there's no end to the flow of ideas and creativity.

theCouponCollection

SOURCEBOOKS, INC.
NAPERVILLE, ILLINOIS

It will always make a Gemini **HAPPY**
to hear the wind in the trees.
Put up a wind chime and enjoy
the **BEAUTIFUL SOUNDS** on a windy day.

A free-spirited Gemini can help an intense, introverted Scorpio to open up, while the Scorpio's dark sensuality can bring emotional depth to the life of the cool Gemini.

theCouponCollection

SOURCEBOOKS, INC
NAPERVILLE, ILLINOIS

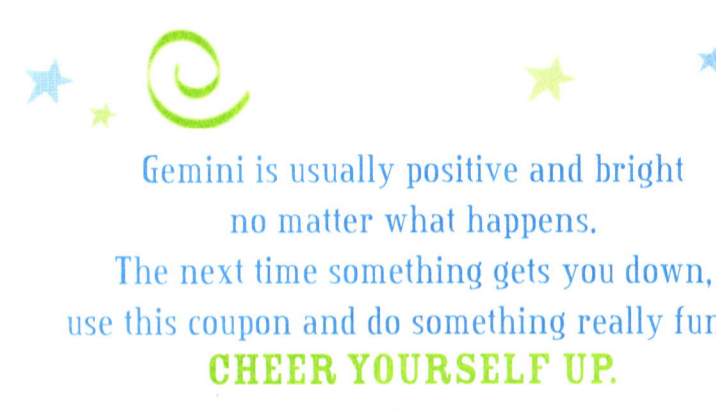

Gemini is usually positive and bright
no matter what happens.
The next time something gets you down,
use this coupon and do something really fun to
CHEER YOURSELF UP.

Gemini, find yourself an optimistic, freedom-loving Sagittarius, and you'll never stop having fun.

theCouponCollection

SOURCEBOOKS, INC.
NAPERVILLE, ILLINOIS

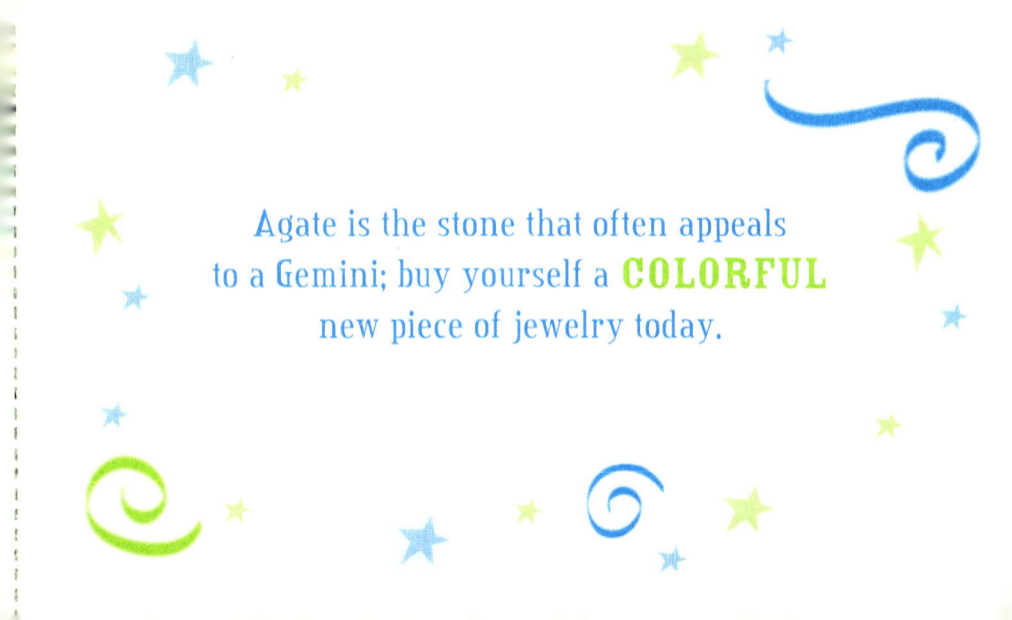

Agate is the stone that often appeals to a Gemini; buy yourself a **COLORFUL** new piece of jewelry today.

Signs of the Zodiac have long been associated with certain gems, metals, animals, flowers, and even herbs and spices.

theCouponCollection
Sourcebooks, Inc.
Naperville, Illinois

Treat yourself to a **SOOTHING** menthol steam and take care of those **DELICATE** Gemini lungs.

Each Zodiac sign is said to rule a particular part of the body—Gemini rules the lungs and shoulders.

theCouponCollection

SOURCEBOOKS, INC.
NAPERVILLE, ILLINOIS

With this coupon, you're entitled to learn to whistle or to play a **WIND INSTRUMENT** like the flute or clarinet.

Libra loves harmony of all kinds, and often enjoys playing music; Gemini and Libra make beautiful music together!

theCouponCollection

The next time you need some calming down,
this coupon entitles you to do some long, deep yoga
breathing. Lie down on your back on the floor,
put your hand over your belly, and feel it rise and fall
as you inhale deeply and exhale slowly.

Gemini and the serious Capricorn will balance each other perfectly.

theCouponCollection

SOURCEBOOKS, INC.
NAPERVILLE, ILLINOIS

Flaunt that **EXUBERANT** Gemini energy—go out dancing.

When an outgoing Gemini teams up with a sociable Sagittarius, chances are good you'll enjoy the company of lots of friends.

theCouponCollection

With this coupon, **INDULGE** yourself
on a hot-air balloon ride.
You'll be right in your element!

An adventurous, passionate Aries would love to sail off into the wild blue yonder with an airy Gemini.

theCouponCollection
SOURCEBOOKS, INC.
NAPERVILLE, ILLINOIS

Bring a **LITTLE FIRE** into your airy existence—try wearing red, yellow, and orange.

The strong, warm-hearted fire sign Leo with the sunny disposition is fascinated and challenged by the quicksilver Gemini.

theCouponCollection

SOURCEBOOKS, INC.

Jump on a trampoline—it's the closest you can **GET TO FLYING!**

Free-spirited Geminis are full of surprises, making them lots of fun to be around.

theCouponCollection

SOURCEBOOKS, INC.
NAPERVILLE, ILLINOIS

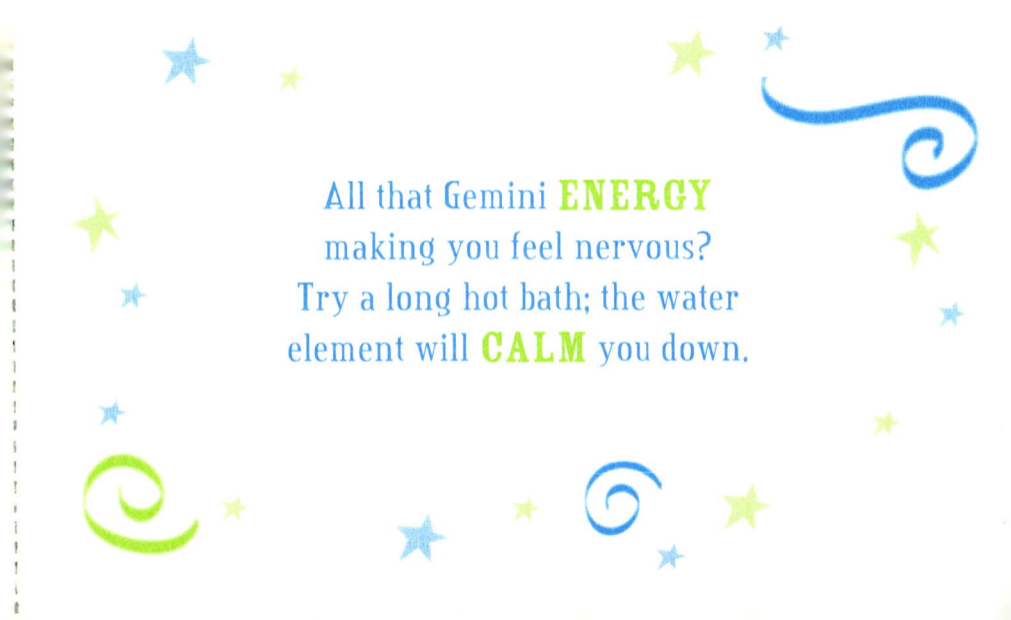

All that Gemini **ENERGY**
making you feel nervous?
Try a long hot bath; the water
element will **CALM** you down.

A water sign like the reserved but passionate Scorpio can be just what Geminis need to balance their energy.

theCouponCollection
Sourcebooks, Inc.
Naperville, Illinois

Gemini is the **COMMUNICATOR**—take this opportunity to send a letter or email to someone you haven't seen in a long time.

Sometimes those close to a free-spirited Gemini need reassurance that your love of independence doesn't mean you don't care about them.

theCouponCollection

SOURCEBOOKS, INC.
NAPERVILLE, ILLINOIS

You're **OUTGOING AND FRIENDLY**—go out
and meet someone new today.

Gemini, find yourself a radiant, generous Leo who will bring out your finest qualities.

theCouponCollection
SOURCEBOOKS, INC.

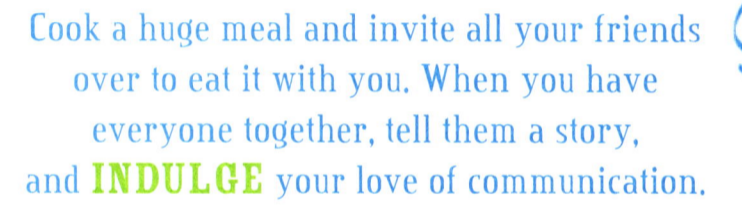

Cook a huge meal and invite all your friends over to eat it with you. When you have everyone together, tell them a story, and **INDULGE** your love of communication.

A loving Taurus can provide the security and sensuous comfort that Geminis might tend to miss out on.

theCouponCollection

SOURCEBOOKS, INC.
NAPERVILLE, ILLINOIS

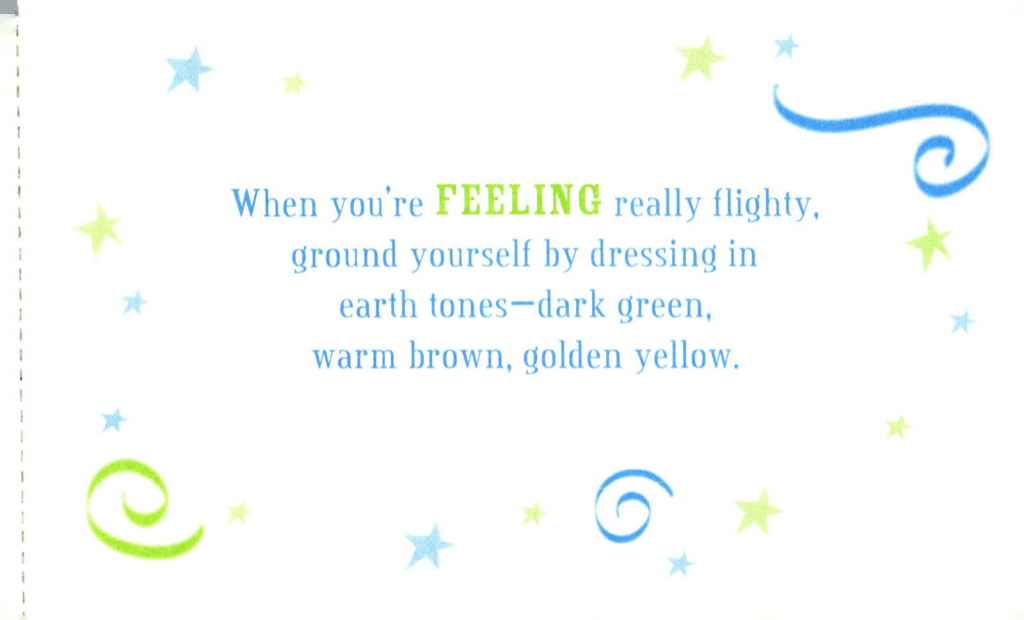

When you're **FEELING** really flighty,
ground yourself by dressing in
earth tones—dark green,
warm brown, golden yellow.

The company of a Capricorn can help keep Gemini firmly rooted in the Earth— when the restless Gemini so desires.

theCouponCollection
SOURCEBOOKS, INC.

Your **MUTABLE NATURE** makes you want to change things around—today, just sit down in the middle of your living room and enjoy the current furniture arrangement. You can always change it again tomorrow!

A gentle Virgo will be sure to keep the Gemini's home environment in perfect order.

theCouponCollection

Earthy activities **COUNTERBALANCE** feelings of insecurity. Pick up some acrylic paints and paint a rock for a doorstop.

A reliable, comfort-loving Taurus is the perfect companion for a Gemini who's looking for a little security.

theCouponCollection

SOURCEBOOKS, INC.
NAPERVILLE, ILLINOIS

The next time it rains, bring the water
and earth elements together to **GROUND YOU**—
take off your shoes and
walk barefoot in a mud puddle.

Air signs like Gemini rely on Earth signs for practical support and Water signs for emotional support.

theCouponCollection
SOURCEBOOKS, INC.
NAPERVILLE, ILLINOIS

Bringing fire into your environment can make it even more volatile, but once in a while it's **EXCITING.** Tonight, eat dinner by candlelight. If you want to go all out, light the whole house with candles.

Gemini will adore the company of the golden Leo with the radiant personality.

theCouponCollection
SOURCEBOOKS, INC.
NAPERVILLE, ILLINOIS

This coupon entitles you to go out on an **UNCONVENTIONAL** date—you pick the time, place, and event.

A Gemini finds great enjoyment in love and romance, as long as they can maintain a certain amount of independence—an Aquarius won't mind this a bit.

theCouponCollection

SOURCEBOOKS, INC.
NAPERVILLE, ILLINOIS

This coupon entitles you to relax after a stressful day. Re-pot some houseplants, or weed your garden. These activities will **SOOTHE YOUR BUSY MIND.**

A warm and sensual
Taurus will tend to
keep the flighty
Gemini firmly
connected.

theCouponCollection

Use your **OUTGOING NATURE** to make
other people feel more comfortable.
Today go and welcome
a new neighbor or co-worker.
With you as the instigator,
the conversation will be lively.

A Gemini can look to the company of the intellectual Aquarius for stimulating conversation.

theCouponCollection
SOURCEBOOKS, INC.
NAPERVILLE, ILLINOIS

Sometimes you make so many plans
that there isn't time for everything.
This coupon entitles you to **PARE DOWN** your
To Do list to only a few items today.
Delegate or forget about the rest.

A powerful Leo can teach Gemini a great deal about tactful delegation and skillful organization.

theCouponCollection
SOURCEBOOKS, INC.
NAPERVILLE, ILLINOIS

To get you **CENTERED**,
do some sit ups.
Remember to breathe!

Let an affectionate Libra help you put balance and harmony in your life.

theCouponCollection
Sourcebooks, Inc.
Naperville, Illinois

Gemini always likes to be outside.
On the next warm evening,
TAKE A PICNIC TO THE PARK.

That kind, sensitive Cancer would love to share a meal with a fascinating Gemini, and Cancer is the best cook in the Zodiac!

theCouponCollection
SOURCEBOOKS, INC.
NAPERVILLE, ILLINOIS

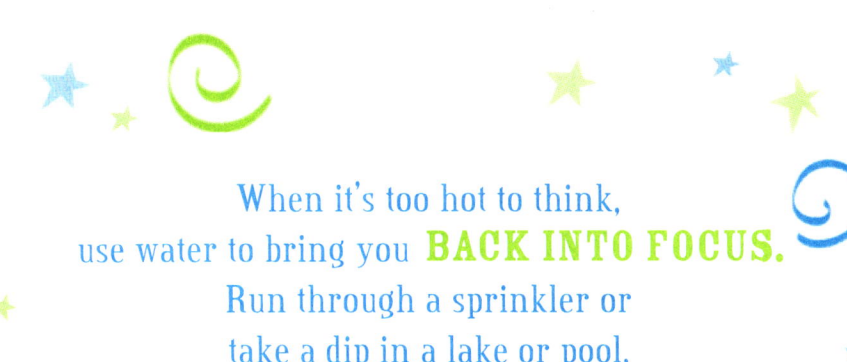

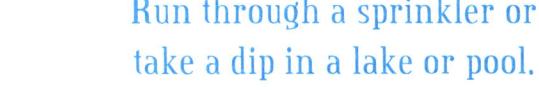

When it's too hot to think,
use water to bring you **BACK INTO FOCUS.**
Run through a sprinkler or
take a dip in a lake or pool.

Gemini will find the company of a quirky Pisces very refreshing.

theCouponCollection

SOURCEBOOKS, INC.
NAPERVILLE, ILLINOIS

This coupon entitles you to **SLOW DOWN** just for a minute. Take five deep breaths, then go back to what you were doing.

Look to a charming Taurus when you want some peace and comfort.

theCouponCollection
SOURCEBOOKS, INC.
NAPERVILLE, ILLINOIS

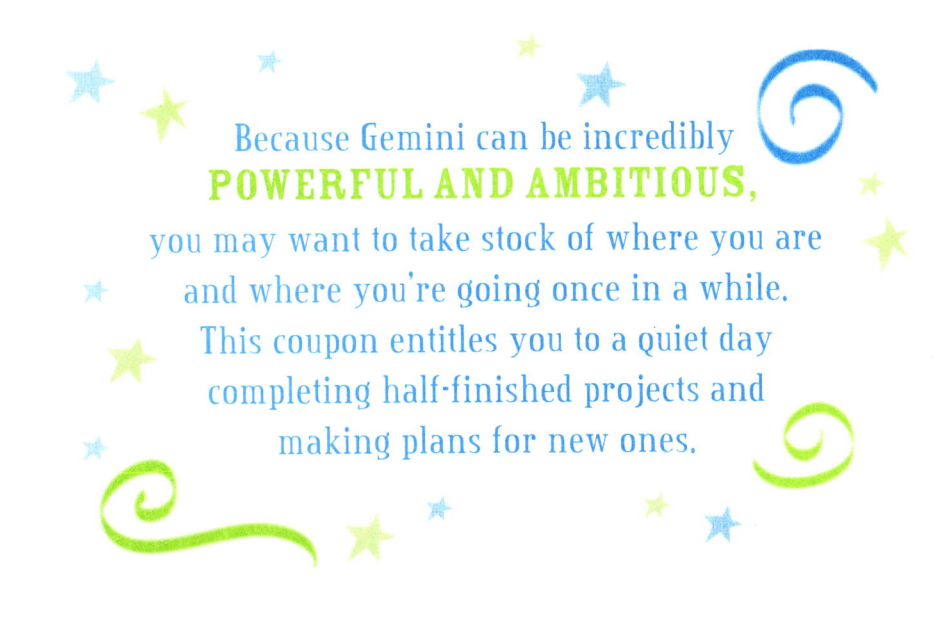

Because Gemini can be incredibly **POWERFUL AND AMBITIOUS,** you may want to take stock of where you are and where you're going once in a while. This coupon entitles you to a quiet day completing half-finished projects and making plans for new ones.

The intense Scorpio is brilliant at pursuing a goal with almost obsessive tenacity—a quality Gemini could use a little more of.

theCouponCollection
SOURCEBOOKS, INC.
NAPERVILLE, ILLINOIS